God's Answers for Today's Problems

KAY ARTHUR
PETE DE LACY

HARVEST HOUSE PUBLISHERS

EUGENE, OREGON

Cover by Koechel Peterson & Associates, Inc., Minneapolis, Minnesota

GOD'S ANSWERS FOR TODAY'S PROBLEMS
Copyright © 2007 by Precept Ministries International
Published by Harvest House Publishers
Eugene, Oregon 97402
www.harvesthousepublishers.com

Arthur, Kay, 1933–
  God's answers for today's problems / Kay Arthur and Pete De Lacy.
      p. cm.—(The new inductive study series)
  Includes bibliographical references.
  ISBN 978-0-7369-1271-6 (pbk.)
  1. Bible. O.T. Proverbs—Textbooks. I. De Lacy, Pete. II. Title
  BS1467.A78 2007
  223'.7—dc22

                                                              2006034079

Contents

ꕔꕔꕔꕔ

*H*ow to *G*et *S*tarted...

Reading directions is sometimes difficult and hardly ever enjoyable! Most often you just want to get started. Only if all else fails will you read the instructions. We understand, but please don't approach this study that way. These brief instructions are a vital part of getting started on the right foot! These few pages will help you immensely.

FIRST

As you study Proverbs, you will need four things in addition to this book:

1. A Bible that you are willing to mark in. The marking is essential. An ideal Bible for this purpose is *The New Inductive Study Bible (NISB)*. The *NISB* is in a single-column text format with large, easy-to-read type, which is ideal for marking. The margins of the text are wide and blank for note taking.

The *NISB* also has instructions for studying each book of the Bible, but it does not contain any commentary on the text, nor is it compiled from any theological stance. Its purpose is to teach you how to discern truth for yourself through the inductive method of study. (The various charts and maps that you will find in this study guide are taken from the *NISB*.)

Whichever Bible you use, just know you will need to mark in it, which brings us to the second item you will need...

2. A fine-point, four-color ballpoint pen or various colored fine-point pens that you can use to write in your Bible. Office supply stores should have those.

3. Colored pencils or an eight-color leaded Pentel pencil.

4. A composition book or a notebook for working on your assignments or recording your insights.

SECOND

1. As you study Proverbs, you will be given specific instructions for each day's study. These should take you between 20 and 30 minutes a day, but if you spend more time than this, you will increase your intimacy with the Word of God and the God of the Word.

If you are doing this study in a class and you find the lessons too heavy, simply do what you can. To do a little is better than to do nothing. Don't be an all-or-nothing person when it comes to Bible study.

Remember, anytime you get into the Word of God, you enter into more intensive warfare with the devil (our enemy). Why? Every piece of the Christian's armor is related to the Word of God. And our one and only offensive weapon is the sword of the Spirit, which is the Word of God. The enemy wants you to have a dull sword. Don't cooperate! You don't have to!

2. As you read each chapter, train yourself to ask the "5 W's and an H": who, what, when, where, why, and how. Asking questions like these helps you see exactly what the Word of God is saying. When you interrogate the text with the 5 W's and an H, you ask questions like these:

a. **What** is the chapter about?

b. **Who** are the main characters?

   c. **When** does this event or teaching take place?

   d. **Where** does this happen?

   e. **Why** is this being done or said?

   f. **How** did it happen?

3. In most of the books in the New Inductive Study Series, we recommend that you mark biblical references to chronology (time) and geography (location) so that you can determine the context of each passage. However, these are not critical for understanding the book of Proverbs, so we won't ask you to mark these in this study.

4. You will be given certain key words to mark throughout Proverbs. This is the purpose of the colored pencils and the colored pens. If you will develop the habit of marking your Bible in this way, you will find it will make a significant difference in the effectiveness of your study and in how much you remember.

A **key word** is an important word that the author uses repeatedly in order to convey his message to his reader. Certain key words will show up throughout each book; others will be concentrated in specific chapters or segments of a book. When you mark a key word, you should also mark its synonyms (words that mean the same thing in the context) and any pronouns *(he, his, she, her, it, we, they, us, our, you, their, them)* in the same way you have marked the key word. We will give you suggestions for ways to mark key words in your daily assignments.

You can use colors or symbols or a combination of colors and symbols to mark words for easy identification. However, colors are easier to distinguish than symbols. When we use symbols, we keep them very simple. For example, you could draw a purple cloud around the word *wisdom* and lightly shade the inside of the cloud like this: **wisdom** .

When marking key words, mark them in a way that is easy for you to remember.

If you devise a color-coding system for marking key words throughout your Bible, then when you look at the pages of your Bible, you will see instantly where a key word is used.

You might want to make yourself a bookmark listing the words you want to mark along with their colors and/or symbols. We will mention some specific key words to watch for in each chapter of Proverbs, but you might consider watching out for these and marking them from the beginning:

> adulteress, harlot, woman of folly
>
> commandment, instruction, knowledge, teaching, understanding
>
> evil, iniquity, sin, wicked, wickedness, abomination
>
> fool, evil
>
> humble, humility
>
> lazy, laziness, sluggard
>
> mouth, words, lips, tongue, gentle answer, harsh word, speech
>
> poor, poverty
>
> pride, proud, arrogant, wise in his own eyes
>
> righteous
>
> wealth, riches
>
> wine, strong drink
>
> wise, wisdom

5. A PROVERBS AT A GLANCE chart is included on page 107. As you complete your study of each chapter,

record the main theme of that chapter under the appropriate chapter number. The main theme of a chapter is what the chapter deals with the most. It may be a particular subject or teaching.

If you will fill out the PROVERBS AT A GLANCE chart as you progress through the study, you will have a complete synopsis of Proverbs when you are finished. If you have a *New Inductive Study Bible*, you will find the same chart in your Bible (page 1061). If you record your chapter themes there, you will have them for a ready reference.

6. Always begin your study with prayer. As you do your part to handle the Word of God accurately, you must remember that the Bible is a divinely inspired book. The words that you are reading are truth, given to you by God so you can know Him and His ways more intimately. These truths are divinely revealed.

> For to us God revealed them through the Spirit; for the Spirit searches all things, even the depths of God. For who among men knows the thoughts of a man except the spirit of the man which is in him? Even so the thoughts of God no one knows except the Spirit of God (1 Corinthians 2:10-11).

Therefore ask God to reveal His truth to you as He leads and guides you into all truth. He will if you will ask.

7. Each day when you finish your lesson, meditate on what you saw. Ask your heavenly Father how you should live in light of the truths you have just studied. At times, depending on how God has spoken to you through His Word, you might even want to wirite LFL ("Lessons for Life") in the margin of your Bible and then, as briefly as possible, record the lesson for life that you want to remember.

THIRD

This study is set up so that you have an assignment for every day of the week—so that you are in the Word daily. If you work through your study in this way, you will find it more profitable than doing a week's study in one sitting. Pacing yourself this way allows time for thinking through what you learn on a daily basis!

The seventh day of each week differs from the other six days. The seventh day is designed to aid group discussion; however, it's also profitable if you are studying this book individually.

The "seventh" day is whatever day in the week you choose to finish your week's study. On this day, you will find a verse or two for you to memorize and Store in Your Heart. Then there is a passage to Read and Discuss. This will help you focus on a major truth or major truths covered in your study that week.

To assist those using the material in a Sunday school class or a group Bible study, there are Questions for Discussion or Individual Study. Even if you are not doing this study with anyone else, answering these questions would be good for you.

If you are in a group, be sure every member of the class, including the teacher, supports his or her answers and insights from the Bible text itself. Then you will be handling the Word of God accurately. As you learn to see what the text says and compare Scripture with Scripture, the Bible explains itself.

Always examine your insights by carefully observing the text to see what it *says*. Then, before you decide what the passage of Scripture *means*, make sure that you interpret it in the light of its context. Scripture will never contradict Scripture. If it ever seems to contradict the rest of the Word of God, you can be certain that something is being taken out of context. If you come to a passage that is difficult to understand, reserve your interpretations for a time when you can study the passage in greater depth.

The purpose of the THOUGHT FOR THE WEEK is to share with you what we consider to be an important element in your week of study. We have included it for your evaluation and, hopefully, for your edification. This section will help you see how to walk in light of what you learned.

Books in the New Inductive Study Series are survey courses. If you want to do a more in-depth study of a particular book of the Bible, we suggest you do a Precept Upon Precept Bible study course on that book. You may obtain more information on these courses by contacting Precept Ministries International at 800-763-8280, visiting our website at www.precept.org, or filling out and mailing the response card in the back of this book.

GOD'S ANSWERS FOR TODAY'S PROBLEMS

∾∾∾∾

What do Jeanne Phillips (also known as Abigail Van Buren), Dr. Laura Schlessinger, and Dr. Phil McGraw have in common?

They all give advice! People want to know how to solve their problems, how to have better lives. Their many stories reveal that the world is full of people with foolish ideas about how to live. Their lives are a mess, so they turn to professionals who seem to have all the answers, who have it together, who have a great deal of success in life.

But are *their* answers really the best? How can we know? What if Dr. Laura and Dr. Phil disagree? Who's right? Are their answers based on their personal experiences? Where do these so-called experts turn when they need advice? Whom do they get their answers from, and how do we know those experts are right?

The debate over who's right has played since the garden of Eden, when Satan questioned what God said to Adam and Eve and even accused Him of not telling them the truth. Since that day, man hasn't stopped looking for truth, though today many people doubt that objective, absolute truth exists at all. Some call our era the postmodern age, in which truth is relative to the individual, to whatever *you* think is true. Accordingly, Dr. Laura and Dr. Phil dispense *their* versions of truth to answer every kind of question and solve every problem.

How do we move from their truth to our truth? What makes us think their experiences will be ours? (We already know we don't have their money!) Are we supposed to process what they say uncritically? How do we know they're right, and what if we disagree? How do we know truth comes from the confusion we call *experience* at all?

And what about our dependency on these gurus? If we live our lives in this world according to their truths, what kind of life will we have? What happens when they quit broadcasting or stop writing books? Will their advice last forever? Will it stand the test of time?

Paul told the Corinthian church that he spoke wisdom "not of this age nor of the rulers of this age, who are passing away; but...God's wisdom" (1 Corinthians 2:6-7). He claimed God's wisdom was different from man's—as different as temporary is from eternal. What a claim—wisdom for all ages! That means past generations had access to it; they didn't lose out because they didn't live long enough to hear from our twenty-first-century experts. This wisdom has always been available to everyone, and now it's here for us.

A thousand years before Paul wrote, God appointed Solomon king over Israel and made him wiser than any man who had ever lived. Solomon's threat to cut a baby in half to determine its real mother has become well-known even to those who don't read the Bible. Such wisdom is recognized as beyond the reasoning of any man. Who could have naturally conceived such an idea?

God chose Solomon, Paul, and other faithful servants to record His supernatural wisdom. Some of this wisdom is captured in the book of Proverbs. Though recorded nearly 3000 years ago, these wise sayings are truths for all times.

Because they're God's timeless truths, they show us how to live wisely in our day, even as our culture changes with the coming and going of the Dr. Lauras and Dr. Phils.

Isaiah 40:8 says, "The word of our God stands forever." God's proverbs give us timeless answers to yesterday's problems, today's problems, and tomorrow's problems. And so as we begin, consider this advice: "Stop regarding man, whose breath of life is in his nostrils; for why should he be esteemed?" (Isaiah 2:22). Only the immortal God can give immortal truth.

PROVERBS

INTRODUCTION TO
PROVERBS

The Bible is made up of 66 distinct books of varying lengths and styles, written by different authors over many years for different purposes. Yet in spite of this variety, the Bible itself says all of it is God-breathed and "profitable for teaching, for reproof, for correction, for training in righteousness" (2 Timothy 3:16). That means it teaches us truth beginning to end, showing us how we've either fallen short of God's ideals or just plain rebelled against His Law, how to get back to where we need to be, and then how to live in a right relationship to God.

The book of Proverbs will show you these things if you study it, carry it around with you in your heart, and live by it. In common usage, the word *proverb* means a saying; a popular, common idea that rings true to life over a range of circumstances. We use many proverbs in ordinary speech. They vary somewhat from culture to culture, and many are consistent with biblical teaching. For example, Benjamin Franklin published "a penny saved is a penny earned" in *Poor Richard's Almanac.* "A rolling stone gathers no moss" promotes activity instead of lethargy (compare Proverbs 6:9-11; 10:4; 13:4; 21:25). "A fool and his money are soon parted" warns us about excessive consumption (see Proverbs 13:18; 23:21). "A stitch in time saves nine" urges us to get a jump on things and avoid procrastination (as do Proverbs 20:13 and 28:19). "A rotten apple spoils the whole bunch" advises us to watch the company we keep (see Proverbs 22:24; 1 Corinthians 5:11; 15:33).

Get the picture? These sayings generally agree with our experience. Many use metaphors, like the rolling stone and the stitch. The saying is literally true—a single stitch early on will keep a tear from enlarging so much that it needs many—but the principle behind it is applicable to dozens of other situations. This is a general principle, not a universal one. It doesn't promise that every single stitch now will save nine stitches later or that no stitching now will demand nine stitches later. Rather, it espouses the general principle that putting off repair now will likely require more repair later (possibly at more time and expense).

Biblical proverbs are the same—they are general principles and not universal promises. Understanding this will prevent much heartache when "promises" don't come true. The proverbs in the book of Proverbs are timeless principles to follow. These guidelines for wise decision making will help you live God's life for you to its fullest. In this foolish world, living wisely is a challenge; we all need help. What better help than God's proverbs for life?

When observing these principles in Proverbs, we need to understand the kind of literature we're reading. The Jews break up their *Tanakh* (Hebrew Bible) into *Torah* (Law), *Nevi'im* (Prophets), and *Kethuvim* (Writings). The book of Proverbs falls within the *Kethuvim*—wise sayings.

Accordingly, Christian Bibles classify Proverbs as wisdom literature and poetry. The main characteristic of Hebrew poetry is parallelism rather than rhyme or meter as in English poetry. Two lines in a verse address the same subject, sometimes comparing, sometimes contrasting. As you read, note the line that explains or amplifies the preceding, says it with a different description or metaphor, or shows its opposite.

KNOWLEDGE, WISDOM, AND FOOLS

Those who lived before us passed down their wisdom to us in the form of short sayings called proverbs. Wisdom is knowledge rightly applied. Without wisdom, we're all fools—our decisions are foolish, and we live foolishly. Unlike the proverbs of men, which are accumulations of human experiences from the world's perspective on success, the book of Proverbs gives us God's wisdom for right living and eternal success...so we don't live like fools.

DAY ONE

Read the first seven verses of Proverbs 1, identify the author, and list his purposes for writing proverbs. Then ask this question: Do I want this? Examine your heart. Do you want what these verses offer? If not, close the book and give it away to someone. You've admitted you're happy being a fool.

If you do want what Proverbs offers, then get ready to dig in and join all those who have sought God's wisdom to live wisely, righteously, justly, and prudently.

Now read the first seven verses again and mark references to *wise* or *wisdom* with a purple cloud shaded light purple. Put a red box around *fools* and shade the box in green.

Shade *instruction, knowledge,* and *understanding*[1] in purple, and marking references to *the LORD* with a purple triangle shaded yellow. What are the relationships among wisdom, fools, and the Lord?

You'll be marking these same words throughout Proverbs, so use a 3 x 5 card as a bookmark, and each week, lesson by lesson, write your key words on it and show how you plan to mark them. Do the same from chapter to chapter. This will help you mark consistently and save time.

How do *instruction, knowledge,* and *understanding* relate to wisdom?

Now, read verses 8-19 and underline the phrase *my son.* How do you think this phrase relates to the author and his purpose for writing?

Who are the adversaries of "my son"? What is their intent? What will be their end?

DAY TWO

Throughout Proverbs, *wisdom* and *fool* are personified. Personification is the literary device that treats inanimate objects as persons and gives them a voice. So pronouns such as *me, my, I,* and *you* are references to whatever is personified. With that in mind, read verses 20-33 and mark *wisdom* and *fools* as before, including any pronouns that refer to them.

What contrast do you find in this section?

Mark the reference to *the LORD* as before and note the truth in this section that parallels the truth in verse 7.

How does the person without wisdom end up? Why does he suffer this fate? List the characteristics that contribute to this end.

DAY THREE

As you continue in this chapter and others, knowing some Hebrew terms might be helpful.

Three Hebrew words are translated *fool* in Proverbs. *Kesiyl* is the dull, closed, stubborn mind that rejects information from others. *Nabal* means no spiritual perception. David's wife Abigail was once married to a man named Nabal, and the name described him perfectly (1 Samuel 25). *Eviyl* (pronounced ev-eel) is an arrogant, flippant, mentally dull, coarse, and callous person.

Now, armed with this information, read Proverbs 1. The fool in verse 7 is *eviyl,* and the fool in verses 22 and 32 is *kesil.* How does this help you understand these texts?

Another enlightening Hebrew term is the one translated *naive* or *simpleminded: pethiy* means simple, foolish, open-minded to the point of naïveté.

If you have Bible study software or word study books, you can look these words up yourself as you study. Meanwhile, we'll point them out when we think they'll help you understand the text better.

Determine a theme for Proverbs 1 and record it on PROVERBS AT A GLANCE on page 107.

DAY FOUR

Today read Proverbs 2:1-5, marking references to *wisdom* and *the* LORD (including *God*) as you have before. Continue to mark *knowledge* and *understanding,* and mark *commandment* the same way, noting how they relate to wisdom. Add them to your bookmark.

What do you learn from marking LORD? How does this fit with Proverbs 1:7?

Read verses 6-11, mark *wisdom, knowledge,* and *understanding* as before, and list the benefits of seeking wisdom as a treasure.

DAY FIVE

Read the rest of Proverbs 2 today, drawing a black cloud around *evil* and *wicked(ness).* Now go back to see how these verses tie in to verses 10 and 11. Underline parallel words.

Now list what you learned about the way of evil. What is the value of wisdom?

DAY SIX

Read Proverbs 2:16-19 and list the characteristics of the strange (immoral) woman.

Now read verses 20-22 and look for conclusions. When do you think these things will happen?

Try outlining the flow of thought in chapter 2. What comes first? What results? What protection is available? How does the chapter conclude?

With these things in mind, determine a theme for Proverbs 2 and record it on PROVERBS AT A GLANCE.

DAY SEVEN

 Store in your heart: Proverbs 1:7
Read and discuss: Proverbs 1–2

Questions for Discussion or Individual Study

- ∾ What's the significance of wisdom and foolishness according to Proverbs 1–2?

- ∾ What kinds of people are discussed in these chapters? Discuss their goals, their kinds of life, and their futures.

- ∾ Discuss the idea of wisdom as treasure.

- ∾ What did you learn about the Lord in these two chapters?

- ∾ How does wisdom protect us?

- ∾ How do wisdom, understanding, knowledge, teaching, and commandments relate to one another?

- ∾ What application can you make to your own life? How does this week's study motivate you?

Thought for the Week

Two friends were walking along the shore of a pond. Suddenly one exclaimed, "Look at how deep those ducks are diving!" She went on to explain that most ducks dabble around in shallow water, feeding from its surface or just below, where food is easy to find. But these ducks plunged into deep waters to find the rich food there.

What an illustration of Proverbs 2:1-5! Most people study the Bible like dabbling ducks, paddling around in shallow water at the edge of the pond, content to feed on grasses and easy prey on the surface or just below, never daring to stray far from the shore. But what if we could be deep divers, venturing out into the deep waters of the Word, diving below the surface to search out the treasure that lies beneath? If we seek wisdom as silver, search for her as for hidden treasure, we will be like ducks that dive deep. We'll "discern the fear of the LORD and discover the knowledge of God" (Proverbs 2:5).

Gaining wisdom takes effort because wisdom *is* deep, and so it needs the deep dive. We need to strive to observe, interpret, and apply God's truth. We won't get wisdom by paddling around in shallow waters, at the pond's edge, looking for effortless meals. We must first believe what God says about wisdom—that it is a treasure—and then desire to have *that* treasure as our most precious treasure. Only then will we be willing to dive deep into the waters.

The effort we're willing to expend to attain something is a measure of how much we value it. We may merely admire something and make no effort to attain it. We may say something is valuable to someone else but never attempt to acquire it for ourselves. We're content to live without it. This is the real measuring stick of our value system—what we're willing to live without and what we're willing to acquire through sacrifice.

Jesus said, "Do not store up for yourselves treasures on earth, where moth and rust destroy, and where thieves break in and steal. But store up for yourselves treasures in heaven, where neither moth nor rust destroys, and where thieves do not break in or steal" (Matthew 6:19-20).

In affluent societies, most people amass great quantities of things that please them, things that moth and rust can destroy and thieves can steal. They don't naturally seek the eternal treasure no creature can take from them—knowledge of God and wisdom.

In poor, oppressed societies, people are forced to look for treasure somewhere else. They already live without most of the worldly goods many of us take for granted. They travel several days to attend Bible studies; we drive to a home group in a few minutes. They give up eating for a week to finance their travel; we may spend the equivalent of our daily latte. Many of them have a better perspective on Matthew 6:19-20 than we have. They model the ducks that dive deep. We can learn a lot by watching them.

THE TEACHING OF A FATHER

According to Deuteronomy 6, Moses gave Israel the commandments so that they, their sons, and their grandsons would fear the Lord and keep all His statutes and commandments all the days of their lives. Moses instructed Israel to teach the commandments diligently to their sons and talk about them all the time—when they sat, walked around, lay down, and rose up.

Less than five hundred years later, Solomon obeyed this command with the hope that through the wisdom God gave him, his son might also fear the Lord.

DAY ONE

Today read Proverbs 3:1-12, marking references to *God* and the key words and phrases *wise, teaching, commandment, understanding, heart,* and *my son.* Then read the section again to determine which verses present matching principles the father gives his son. Watch for the word *so,* which introduces the reason for the instruction that precedes it.

Make a list of the instructions and principles in these verses. Beside each one, list the result or the value of following the principle. You may want to rephrase principles to firm up your understanding, and memorizing your words will help you. Over the course of these 13 weeks, you'll see many principles repeated, giving you an idea of how important God thinks they are for us to know.

DAY TWO

Read Proverbs 3:13-20 and continue with the directions (including noting key words and phrases) from yesterday. Make sure to mark *wisdom* and references to *the LORD*. Watch for pronouns and synonyms.

List all you learn about wisdom.

Compare the list of instructions and principles from yesterday with today's list about wisdom. Notice that these verses are not instructions, but they do contain principles for living.

DAY THREE

Read Proverbs 3:21-35 today, marking key words, including *my son*, *wisdom (wise)*, and references to *the LORD*. Continue looking for verses grouped around similar principles and subsequent good and bad consequences.

How do verses 27-30 relate to verses 31-35?

Finally, determine the theme of Proverbs 3 and record it on PROVERBS AT A GLANCE on page 107.

DAY FOUR

Read Proverbs 4:1-9 today, marking *my son (O sons)*, *heart*, *instruction (teaching)*, *understanding*,[2] *commandments*, and *wisdom*. These key words appear throughout Proverbs. Consider starting a running list of everything you learn about these words throughout your study of the book of Proverbs. Several other themes run through the book, so as you see them cropping up again and again, you can compile lists of everything you learn in all the chapters of Proverbs.

Now go back and read Proverbs 1:1 and note the author. Read Proverbs 4:3; 2 Samuel 12:14,24; and 1 Chronicles 14:3-4. Can you figure out the author's father and mother? Was he the only son of his mother?

In light of these verses, what does "the only son in the sight of my mother" mean? What do you think?

What actions does the author urge? Make a list, and as before, write out the benefits for each action in a second column.

Do you want these benefits?

DAY FIVE

Read Proverbs 4:10-19 today, marking *my son*, *wisdom*, and *wicked*. Again, list instructions for and benefits of seeking wisdom.

Also list instructions regarding avoiding wickedness, and separately list characteristics of the wicked.

Contrast the wicked and the righteous. (Hint: Look for the word *but*.) Contrasts are very important in Proverbs. If you don't understand an instruction, the contrast may make it clear.

DAY SIX

For our last day of study, read Proverbs 4:20-27, again marking *my son* and *heart*.

Note the instructions about "my sayings" or "my words" and their value to those who find them.

Now list the body parts the author mentions and the instructions for each one. Summarize how they relate to verse 22.

Don't forget to determine a theme for Proverbs 4 and record it on PROVERBS AT A GLANCE.

DAY SEVEN

Store in your heart: Proverbs 3:5-6
Read and discuss: Proverbs 3–4

QUESTIONS FOR DISCUSSION OR INDIVIDUAL STUDY

∞ Discuss the father-son relationship implied in Proverbs 3–4. Does it apply to women too?

∞ What are the benefits of acquiring wisdom?

∞ What are the qualities or characteristics of wisdom?

∞ What is the relationship between the son who acquires wisdom and the Lord?

- ∾ Contrast the righteous and the wicked.

- ∾ Summarize the central teachings of these two chapters and discuss how you can remember them.

Thought for the Week

Although Solomon had 700 wives and 300 concubines, only one son is named—Rehoboam, who succeeded Solomon as king of Israel. We don't know whether "my son" is a reference to Rehoboam or someone else. We *do* know that the principle of fathers passing wisdom to their sons is biblical. We've already seen this in Proverbs 4:1-5, and we know it from the Lord's command to pass the (Mosaic) Law down:

> Now this is the commandment, the statutes and the judgments which the LORD your God has commanded me to teach you, that you might do them in the land where you are going over to possess it, so that you and your son and your grandson might fear the LORD your God, to keep all His statutes and His commandments which I command you, all the days of your life, and that your days may be prolonged. O Israel, you should listen and be careful to do it, that it may be well with you and that you may multiply greatly, just as the LORD, the God of your fathers, has promised you, in a land flowing with milk and honey.
>
> Hear, O Israel! The LORD is our God, the LORD is one! You shall love the LORD your God with all your heart and with all your soul and with all your might. These words, which I am commanding you today, shall be on your heart. You shall teach them diligently to your sons and

shall talk of them when you sit in your house
and when you walk by the way and when you
lie down and when you rise up. You shall bind
them as a sign on your hand and they shall be
as frontals on your forehead. You shall write
them on the doorposts of your house and on
your gates (Deuteronomy 6:1-9).

The principle is clear—God's Law is to be part of the
everyday conversation between a father and his son.

The command is repeated in Deuteronomy 32:45-47, just
before Israel enters the promised land:

When Moses had finished speaking all these
words to all Israel, he said to them, "Take to your
heart all the words with which I am warning
you today, which you shall command your sons
to observe carefully, even all the words of this
law. For it is not an idle word for you; indeed it
is your life. And by this word you will prolong
your days in the land, which you are about to
cross the Jordan to possess" (2 Deuteronomy
32:45-47).

One principle is clear: God's Word is life. In order to live,
we have to breathe the breath of life, eat the bread of life. The
wisdom of God is this: "Keep my commandments and live"
(Proverbs 4:4).

A second, clear principle is that fathers must pass this
wisdom on to their sons—father to son, son to grandson,
and so on through the ages.

How this principle has dwindled in modern times! How
we as parents, fathers and mothers, have failed to sit with our
children and discuss the principles of life that stand them in
good stead and keep them from being snared by the wicked,

straying off the path of righteousness. Oh, yes, some have kept up the practice, but many parents have simply given up.

Think about your own upbringing. What did your father or mother hand down to you? Do you recall *any* conversations about the Lord and His wisdom? Life moves so quickly today, and information is so readily available, but do *we* take the time to share the biblical wisdom, stories, and principles the Lord has commanded us to share with our children?

In our industrialized, motorized nations, we travel at speeds ranging from fast to nearly the speed of light—physically in automobiles, trains, and jet aircraft, and cognitively in cell phones and the Internet. Before this latest revolution of e-mail and Internet telephony, we traveled by horse and sat on porches, hearths, or banks of streams and talked. We talked about life, about lessons learned, about common wisdom—father to son, mother to daughter, grandfathers, grandmothers, aunts, and uncles to the younger generations.

I remember my grandfather gently chiding me one day as we cleared brush from a field. I struggled with a large load of freshly cut brush. "You're carrying a lazy man's load," he said. "What's a lazy man's load?" I asked. "The load a man carries when he's too lazy to make two trips," he replied.

I was in elementary school at the time, but the proverb has stuck for 50 years. Today I ask myself if I've been carrying a lazy man's load as I pass on to the next generation the things of life, God's wisdom. Am I trying to get it all done quickly, overloading people with information, giving them too much for one trip?

Today we should reflect on what was once a common practice and ask ourselves, if it was valuable then, isn't it valuable today? David passed God's wisdom on to Solomon, and Solomon passed it on to his son, one proverb at a time, for a lifetime.

As an Ox Goes
to the Slaughter

Enticed by persuasions, seduced by flattering lips, the young man lacking sense is led away by an adulteress like an ox to the slaughter. He doesn't stand a chance because he didn't treat wisdom as his sister or understanding as his friend.

DAY ONE

Read Proverbs 5:1-14 today, marking references to the *adulteress*[3] with a red cloud shaded light red. Add *adulteress* to your bookmark. As in past chapters, also mark *my son*.

Make a list of what you learn about adulteresses. Adultery is a key concept in the Ten Commandments, in the Law, and in the New Testament. A subject that is repeated throughout the Bible is probably a very important topic. Sometimes the Bible uses the word *adultery* literally, referring to physical, sexual sin. At other times, the Bible uses the word *adultery* metaphorically and addresses Israel's tendency to worship other gods. Which subject is being addressed here in Proverbs?

List instructions in one column and positive and negative consequences in a second column.

DAY TWO

Read Proverbs 5:15-23, marking *adulteress* and *the LORD* as you have before, and mark *iniquities (sin)* by shading it brown. Add *iniquities* to your bookmark.

Also note metaphors about water: cisterns, wells, springs, streams, and fountains. Note the instructions. What principle relates to a wife? How does this contrast with the one that relates to an adulteress?

Be sure to note the destiny (the "end") of the wicked. The wicked and the righteous each have a destiny, and as you might expect, one destiny is unpleasant, and one is pleasant. What evil is discussed in this chapter?

Record a theme for Proverbs 5 on PROVERBS AT A GLANCE on page 107.

DAY THREE

Read Proverbs 6:1-19 and mark *my son*, *wise*, and *the LORD*. Then group verses by the subjects they cover. You can use the paragraphs provided in your Bible or group paragraphs together if you think they cover the same subject.

DAY FOUR

Today read Proverbs 6:20-35, marking *adulteress*[4] *(adultery)*, *commandment (teaching)*, and *my son* as before.

List what you learn about the commandment of the father and the teaching of the mother.

Also list what you learn about the adulteress. If you like, make a composite list about the adulteress by adding to what you learned in chapter 5 and continuing to add to it as you study the rest of Proverbs.

What consequences does a man risk by associating with an adulteress?

Record your theme for Proverbs 6 on PROVERBS AT A GLANCE.

DAY FIVE

Today's reading is of Proverbs 7. Mark *wisdom* as you have before. Mark *adulteress*[5] and *harlot*.[6] If *harlot* is a synonym for adulteress, mark it the same way. If not, put a red cloud around it but shade it differently. Also mark *heart, my son(s),* and any synonyms. Put a red heart over the word *heart*.

List what you learn about wisdom. What are the commandments or instructions about wisdom? How are the heart and wisdom related? How do they keep us from making a mistake with adultery?

DAY SIX

Read Proverbs 7:6-23 again and list what you learn about the adulteress and the young man who lacks sense. How does she operate, and what is the result? What price does he pay?

Determine a theme for Proverbs 7 and then record it on PROVERBS AT A GLANCE.

DAY SEVEN

Store in your heart: Proverbs 6:16-19
Read and discuss: Proverbs 5:3-6,15-20; 6:16-19,23-29; 7:6-27

QUESTIONS FOR DISCUSSION OR INDIVIDUAL STUDY

∽ Discuss the central teaching of Proverbs 5–7.

∽ What are some of the tactics of the adulteress?

∽ How is a man vulnerable to these tactics?

∽ How does Proverbs 6:16-19 relate to the teaching about the adulteress?

∽ Discuss how the commandments of the father and teachings of the mother help a naive young man.

∽ How should we respond to God's instruction in these chapters?

THOUGHT FOR THE WEEK

In an agrarian culture, the picture of an ox being led to slaughter said it all. No one needed an explanation to grasp the meaning of the analogy and its corresponding succinct, poetic phrase.

Today, we don't see oxen led to slaughter or birds to snares, but still the idea is crystal clear. Modern statements express the same concept: "He never saw it coming!" "He was blindsided!" "Didn't suspect a thing!" What caused the surprise? Lack of wisdom! And lack of wisdom about adulteresses has never disappeared.

The adulteress' lips still drip honey, and her mouth speaks words smoother than oil just as much today as in Solomon's day. Her enticing logic, her persuasion, her seducing flattery...all the same.

She's still visually attractive: Her form exhilarates, her eyes capture, her dress entices.

Her behavior is ever exciting, boisterous, rebellious; she kisses and embraces and makes promises of sexual favors without fear of being caught.

But she lies. Her house is on the way to *Sheol*; it leads to the chambers of death. The fool will get burned. The jealous husband will not spare in the day of vengeance; he will not accept any ransom. The ox is led to slaughter.

Wisdom reminds us that this is not new. Remember, Solomon's mother was Bathsheba, and his father, David. David well may have taught Solomon these principles from his own experience. One evening, David rose from his bed, walked on the roof of his house, and lingered while he watched the wife of Uriah the Hittite bathing.

She was attractive. He inquired about her. He was enticed. He sent for her. She came. Her husband was away at war; he would never find out. They committed adultery.

Uriah never knew, so he didn't become an enraged, jealous husband. But God acted in his place—*God* didn't "spare in the day of vengeance." Bathsheba's steps led the baby conceived in adultery to Sheol. David was spared. Bathsheba was spared. But their child died. Strife arises in David's house as three of his other sons compete for the throne. The three (Amnon, Absalom, and Adonijah) all die from this rivalry.

A lingering look led to a lustful thought, which led to an improper invitation. Sin, conceived in the heart, took form. And the terrible consequences reached to four of David's sons.

What could have stopped this? Wisdom! Understanding! Obedience to God's commandments: "You shall not commit adultery...You shall not covet your neighbor's wife" (Exodus 20:14,17).

Job 31:31 says, "I have made a covenant with my eyes; how then could I gaze at a virgin?"

"There are six things which the LORD hates, yes, seven which are an abomination to Him" (Proverbs 6:16):

1. haughty eyes
2. lying tongues
3. hands that shed innocent blood
4. a heart that devises wicked plans
5. feet that run rapidly to evil
6. a false witness who utters lies
7. one who spreads strife among brothers (see Proverbs 6:17)

If you read 2 Samuel 11, you'll see that David committed several of these. And he reaped the consequences. Proverbs is designed to keep a man from repeating David's sins—and others. That's why he passed his wisdom to Solomon and Solomon passed them to his son...and to you, to me, and so on.

Write them on the tablet of your heart.

THE CALL OF WISDOM OR OF THE FOOLISH WOMAN

Food and wine are set at wisdom's table, and she calls men to forsake folly and live. But the foolish woman equally calls men to secretly partake of her stolen water and bread...and then die. Can you distinguish these voices? Will you heed the right call?

DAY ONE

Read Proverbs 8 and mark *wisdom,*[7] *knowledge, understanding, love,* and LORD. Mark *blessing* with a purple cloud shaded pink. Add *love* and *blessing* to your bookmark.

In this chapter, wisdom is personified, so you'll find many feminine pronouns. Look for them so you don't miss any significant observations. Personification is a literary device that draws attention to and explains a concept in a way we can relate to. The characteristics of a person are attributed to the concept because we understand how people think and act.

45

DAY TWO

All we need to do today is list the claims wisdom makes in verses 1-21. Take your time and meditate on what you learn in these verses. They're so rich!

DAY THREE

Read verses 22-36 again and list what you learn about the relationship between the Lord and wisdom. As you have seen, true wisdom comes from the Lord. The world's wisdom can never compare to the Lord's wisdom.

As usual, when we come to the end of a chapter, we need to capture its essence by determining a theme and recording it on the AT A GLANCE chart. So today, record the theme for Proverbs 8 on PROVERBS AT A GLANCE on page 107.

DAY FOUR

Read Proverbs 9, marking *wisdom* and *understanding*,[8] and the *woman of folly*.[9] Watch for pronouns referring to these characters.

DAY FIVE

Read Proverbs 9:1-6. List what wisdom has done and the message she calls out.

Now read verses 13-18. List what you learn about the woman of folly and her message.

How does the woman of folly relate to the adulteress and harlot we marked before?

Note the important words in the two invitations and the different results from listening to these words.

DAY SIX

Read verses 7-12 and summarize the wisdom of these verses. You may want to mark *love* (with a red heart shaded red), *wicked, the* LORD, and *life* (with a green cloud shaded green) in these verses. Add *life* to your bookmark.

Compare what you learn about the naive ones in Proverbs 8:5; 9:4; and 9:16. If you don't know what *naive* means, look it up in a dictionary. This understanding will help you see why men need to watch out for women of folly, adulteresses, and harlots. They're all ready to spring a trap.

Determine a theme for Proverbs 9 and record it on PROVERBS AT A GLANCE.

DAY SEVEN

 Store in your heart: Proverbs 9:10
Read and discuss: Proverbs 8–9

QUESTIONS FOR DISCUSSION OR INDIVIDUAL STUDY

∿ What did you learn from wisdom personified?

- ∾ Discuss the contrast between wisdom and the woman of folly.

- ∾ How are wisdom and the Lord related?

- ∾ What results from acquiring wisdom?

- ∾ What results from chasing after foolishness?

- ∾ Why does God favor those who listen to and obey wisdom?

- ∾ Discuss how you can apply what you learned in Proverbs 8–9 to your life today.

THOUGHT FOR THE WEEK

In the parable of the Good Shepherd (John 10), Jesus says the sheep know the voice of the shepherd and follow him, but they will not follow the voice of the stranger because they do not know his voice. How do sheep know their shepherd's voice? Familiarity! The shepherd spends time with them, and they become accustomed to his voice. Even if they don't see him, they hear and come to know his voice. If they hear the voice of a stranger, they know he is not their shepherd, and they flee.

Wisdom calls out to the naive (simple), who need prudence, wisdom, and understanding. The woman of folly calls too, but her purpose is different. Wisdom calls to the naive to forsake folly and live; the woman of folly calls the naive to continue in folly and die, deceiving them with the promises of sweet water and pleasant bread.

How do you know which voice to follow? How can you tell which voice is wisdom and which voice is folly? Familiarity! If you spend time with wisdom, you'll learn to recognize her voice and differentiate it from the voice of the strange woman, folly.

This is Solomon's point so far in nine chapters of Proverbs: Spend time listening to the voice of wisdom. Get to know her voice so you can distinguish it from the voice of folly—especially because both voices entice by promising pleasurable things. Only one voice is telling the truth.

To recognize the voice of wisdom, you must spend time with wisdom. And where is wisdom found? In God's Word—in Proverbs and the other 65 books of the Bible. Spending time in God's Word will teach you the voice of God (the voice of wisdom) and keep you off the path to foolishness and destruction.

In Proverbs 7, Solomon encourages you to call understanding your intimate friend and wisdom your sister. Make wisdom your best friend, your closest relative. This is what Solomon urges and illustrates repeatedly with word pictures. Solomon wants his son to listen to more than *his* words; he wants him to listen to wisdom. He wants him to listen to the wisdom of God, which dwelled at His side as a master workman when the world was created (8:27-31).

Eve listened to the voice of a stranger, not wisdom; to the serpent, not God. The result was death. He who has ears, let him hear the voice of wisdom, the voice of God, and live. Listen to the Word of God, spend time with it, make it your most intimate friend, turn to it and away from the voice of the strange woman of folly. Know the voice well enough so that when enticements sound alike you'll recognize sharply different meanings and consequences and always follow the right voice—the voice of God.

THE MOUTH
OF THE RIGHTEOUS

"Sticks and stones may break my bones, but words will never hurt me" is an age-old childish retort to cruel words spoken. I have a good idea you never believed it and never will. That's because it's false—words *do* hurt! Words can lead astray and kill. Words can also lead aright and generate life. Wicked and righteous words lead in opposite directions to opposite, eternal places.

DAY ONE

Read Proverbs 10 today and mark *wise, wisdom,* and *fool* as you have before. Also mark references to speaking by putting a brown triangle around such words as *mouth, words, lips,* and *tongue,* and add these to your bookmark. The New Testament teaches us much about what comes out of our mouths and how that reveals what is in our hearts.

Read the chapter again and mark *righteous,*[10] *wicked(ness),*[11] *life,* and *death,* and add new key words you find to your bookmark. Mark *righteous* with an *R* and *death* with a black headstone like this:  .

DAY TWO

Now that you've marked key words, you can see that the chapter has more than one topic. List what you learn about the *wise,* the *fool,* the *wicked,* and the *righteous.* As you make these lists you'll see how life, death, and the mouth relate to each group of people.

You may also want to write out the connections between wisdom and the righteous and between foolishness and the wicked. These connections are important—don't miss them!

Proverbs 10:1 mentions the author again and begins a new segment. Mark it on PROVERBS AT A GLANCE on page 107. Also deduce a theme for Proverbs 10 and record it on PROVERBS AT A GLANCE.

DAY THREE

Moving on to Proverbs 11 today, mark the same key words that you marked in chapter 10. Mark *evil* the same way you marked *wicked.*

If you haven't made a bookmark that shows your key words and the way you're marking them, do it now so you'll mark consistently. You'll also find it saves time, giving you more time to consider what you learn. Marking many different key words can become confusing without a consistent system. Consistency is key when you review any book of the

Bible—it shows you the way God uses repetition in His Word to emphasize important teachings.

DAY FOUR

Now that you've marked references to the wicked in Proverbs 11, list what you learn about the wicked (evil) and their future. Contrast these with what you see about the righteous and their destiny so that you see the reason for knowing the difference and choosing the right path.

Determine a theme of Proverbs 11 and record it on PROVERBS AT A GLANCE.

DAY FIVE

Read Proverbs 12 and mark the key words from your bookmark. As you'll see, this chapter continues subjects from chapters 10 and 11. We've built up quite a list of key words, haven't we? Take your time marking. We'll make lists tomorrow.

DAY SIX

List what you learn about wisdom, the fool, the righteous, and the wicked. You may find it helpful to consolidate what you learned from these three chapters about the effects of what people say.

Finally, determine a theme of Proverbs 12 and record it on PROVERBS AT A GLANCE.

DAY SEVEN

Store in your heart: Proverbs 10:20
Read and discuss: Proverbs 10:6-21; 11:1-8; 12:20-28

QUESTIONS FOR DISCUSSION OR INDIVIDUAL STUDY

- ∾ Contrast the actions of the righteous and the wicked.

- ∾ How does what we say affect people?

- ∾ Discuss results of good behavior, such as godly diligence and labor.

- ∾ How do the two kinds of people in these chapters influence others?

- ∾ What applications can you make in your own life from these two kinds of people? What kind of influence do you want to have? To avoid?

- ∾ How do these truths relate to raising children?

THOUGHT FOR THE WEEK

Proverbs teaches that words matter. Lying lips prompted by hatred and deceit lead to ruin and death. The mouth of the wicked is an endless source of trouble, unavoidably expressing the true condition of the heart.

Jesus taught this linkage between the naturally evil heart and its mouthpiece. In Matthew 15:11 He said, "It is not what enters into the mouth that defiles the man, but what proceeds out of the mouth, this defiles the man." In verses 17-19, He explains:

> Do you not understand that everything that goes into the mouth passes into the stomach, and is eliminated? But the things that proceed out of the mouth come from the heart, and those defile the man. For out of the heart come evil thoughts, murders, adulteries, fornications, thefts, false witness, slanders.

Jesus is saying the same thing about the mouth and heart that the Father revealed to Solomon to record in Proverbs. In John 12:49 Jesus said, "For I did not speak on My own initiative, but the Father Himself who sent Me has given Me a commandment as to what to say and what to speak." Jesus taught something the Pharisees could have known from Proverbs and taught themselves. Instead they emphasized dietary regulations of the Law as the way to be holy.

James also teaches us about the tongue:

> But no one can tame the tongue; it is a restless evil and full of deadly poison. With it we bless our Lord and Father, and with it we curse men, who have been made in the likeness of God; from the same mouth come both blessing and cursing. My brethren, these things ought not to be this way. Does a fountain send out from the same opening both fresh and bitter water? Can a fig tree, my brethren, produce olives, or a vine produce figs? Nor can salt water produce fresh (James 3:8-12).

Do you see how this parallels Proverbs? The mouth can utter two kinds of things. Proverbs 10:32 says, "The lips of the righteous bring forth what is acceptable, but the mouth of the wicked what is perverted."

Jesus' in-and-out, out-from-within analogy was aimed at the Pharisees, who spoke things that appeared to be acceptable but actually perverted truth. They taught traditions of men instead of the commandments of God. They taught that what people eat can defile them, because the Law had proscribed certain creatures as unclean. But keeping such rules while ignoring the evil motives of the heart did not make a man holy and acceptable to God. And with their words, the Pharisees led people astray.

James expands on this by adding that a man's words agree with his true character, whether wicked or righteous. So in the long run we can determine a man's general character by his speech.

James continues to parallel Proverbs as he links deeds with two kinds of wisdom—one from above, one from below:

> Who among you is wise and understanding? Let him show by his good behavior his deeds in the gentleness of wisdom. But if you have bitter jealousy and selfish ambition in your heart, do not be arrogant and so lie against the truth. This wisdom is not that which comes down from above, but is earthly, natural, demonic. For where jealousy and selfish ambition exist, there is disorder and every evil thing. But the wisdom from above is first pure, then peaceable, gentle, reasonable, full of mercy and good fruits, unwavering, without hypocrisy. And the seed whose fruit is righteousness is sown in peace by those who make peace (James 3:13-18).

According to Solomon's proverbs, as chapter 10 begins, "A wise son makes a father glad."

Our heavenly Father is glad when He sees wisdom in His children. Jesus and James amply prove that Solomon's proverbs are as true and applicable today as they were when God originally gave that wisdom to Solomon to record for us. God never changes, and His wisdom never changes.

The Teaching of the Wise Is a Fountain of Life

The way of the adulteress, the foolish woman, leads to death; so too, the way of the wicked. But what leads to life? The teaching of the wise and the fear of the Lord.

DAY ONE

The book of Proverbs (and the entire Bible!) often contrasts life and death. Read Proverbs 13 today, marking the key words on your bookmark. Watch for references to life and death. Which dominates this chapter?

DAY TWO

Now list what you learned from marking *wisdom* and *knowledge*, *fools*, *wicked*, and *life*. As we make these lists, we're compiling truth to live by: things to know that affect the way we live.

DAY THREE

Now look at contrasts and comparisons in the chapter (for example, between the wise and the foolish and between the righteous and the wicked) and see what you can discern. Do any general subjects or themes emerge in the chapter?

Finally, record a theme for Proverbs 13 on PROVERBS AT A GLANCE on page 107.

DAY FOUR

Read Proverbs 14 and mark the key words on your bookmark. These may seem repetitive, but we must observe the text before we can understand it.

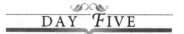

DAY FIVE

List what you learn from the contrast between the wise and the foolish and between the righteous and the wicked.

DAY SIX

Look at the relationship between the mouth, knowledge, understanding, and wisdom. Write out your conclusions. Marking key words and making lists helps us observe the text, but we need to press on to interpretation and application. We need to think through what we see and what we experience so we can draw conclusions. These conclusions become the principles that we live by. Principles that are based on God's teaching can guide our experience and help us avoid unpleasant consequences.

Determine a theme for Proverbs 14 and record it on PROVERBS AT A GLANCE.

DAY SEVEN

Store in your heart: Proverbs 13:12

Read and discuss: Proverbs 13:13-21; 14:1-9,24-33

QUESTIONS FOR DISCUSSION OR INDIVIDUAL STUDY

- Discuss the contrast between the wise and the fool from these chapters.

- What is the relationship between the mouth, knowledge, and wisdom?

- Discuss the relationship of wisdom to life and death and to those who reject it.

- How does the company you keep affect you? What application can you make to your life?

- Discuss verses that really spoke to your heart or ministered to a specific need in your life today.

THOUGHT FOR THE WEEK

Why do you think Solomon said that the teaching of the wise and the fear of the Lord are like a fountain of life and keep us from the snares of death? He's speaking to his living son, isn't he? Don't we all die? What does he mean?

Psalm 90:10 says that the days of our lives reach to 70 or 80 years. Yes, some live longer or shorter lives, and the Bible describes much longer life spans in earlier ages, but the days of man have been limited to these rough numbers from the times of the kings of Israel until today.

The psalmist is contrasting the short life span of man and the eternity of God. Verse 4 of Psalm 90 says that a thousand years to God's sight "are like yesterday when it passes by." Peter echoes this in his second epistle: "But do not let this one fact escape your notice, beloved, that with the Lord one day is like a thousand years, and a thousand years like one day" (2 Peter 3:8). Eternity is so much greater than our short lives, we can't comprehend it—it's too large a concept for mortals to grasp. But God calls us into eternal life.

The wisdom of Solomon calls us to life, not death. It speaks of present behavior as well as long-term conse-quences—eternal life and death. The fear of the Lord, the teaching of the wise, is to believe His Word and to live forever, for all eternity future. When the Word of God says to believe in Him and live, it means to live eternally.

> Jesus said to her, "I am the resurrection and the life; he who believes in Me will live even if he dies, and everyone who lives and believes in Me will never die. Do you believe this?" (John 11:25-26).

Solomon's wisdom helps us live lives that glorify God so that we can enjoy the spiritual riches of life in obedience to God's Word *today*. But all of God's Word ultimately points to His saving grace in the promised seed—the eternal gospel (Revelation 14:6). So when Solomon identifies the choices of wisdom and folly with the choices of life and death, he predictively includes the perfect life and death of the Messiah

(Christ), Jesus of Nazareth, Son of God and Savior—first announced in Genesis 3:15.

With the advent of Christ, the teaching of the truly wise includes the gospel. As Paul explains in 1 Corinthians 1:23-24, Christ crucified is the power and wisdom of God. After God reveals His gospel, the fear of the Lord propels us to believe it.

If we hold to the verbal, plenary inspiration of Scripture—that all Scripture is God-breathed—we know Solomon's wisdom, which leads to life now, necessarily includes faith in Christ, the wisdom and life of God. What could show greater wisdom than believing God's promise of eternal life through faith in Jesus Christ, and what could show greater foolishness than rejecting it?

Wisdom rests in the heart of those who have understanding, but fools display the folly in their hearts. The one with understanding lives quietly by what he knows in his heart. But the fool boasts to others, living without it. Living by Solomon's proverbs is godly living, faith in God's Word as true and His way as right. If we believe God's Word is true and His way is right, we will believe His gospel—His Word of life (1 John 1:1).

If you haven't believed the gospel, all the obedience to Solomon's proverbs you can muster will fall short of eternal life. Once the Father reveals His Son's Person and perfect work, only faith in who He is and what He has done truly fulfills Solomon's guidance for wise living, and only this faith glorifies God.

If you haven't believed the gospel, why don't you do so today? All people are sinners; all of us have sinned, and all of us deserve to die as the just penalty for sin. But Jesus died to pay the penalty of death your sin earns; He was raised from the dead so that you too might pass from death into life spiritually now and be raised physically from the dead later—at the end of the age. All you have to do is believe these things—that you are a sinner, that Jesus died for your sins, and that He was raised for your justification. You must repent (change your mind) and believe that Jesus is exactly who He says He is: God, Son of God, Lord, and Savior.

If you believed today, Beloved, welcome to the family. Praise the Lord! Tell someone about it. Write to Kay or Pete at Precept Ministries International, PO Box 182218, Chattanooga, TN 37422. We have a gift for you to help you in your new life.

PRIDE GOES BEFORE A FALL

ബൈയായ

"Pride goes before a fall" is a common proverb. This week we'll see the full, correct quotation in its context. The New American Standard Bible uses *stumbling* where others use *fall,* but the meaning is the same. Pride plays an important role in the contrast between wisdom and foolishness.

DAY ONE

Read Proverbs 15 today, marking the key words on your bookmark. Also mark *reproof* [12] *(reprove)* and add it to your bookmark. *Reproof* isn't a word we use much today, but the Bible uses it about 20 times. The word means to show someone where they're wrong. We need the Scriptures and other people to help us know when we're wrong so we can change how we think and act. Only when we realize we're wrong are we open to correction and willing to learn how to change for the better.

Perhaps you know 2 Timothy 3:16-17. If not, look up these verses. Remember that Proverbs is part of Scripture.

DAY TWO

Read chapter 15 again today and mark or note references to speaking, like *gentle answer* and *harsh word* the same way you marked *mouth, words, lips,* and *tongue.* Then list what you learn about speaking and its effect. James has much to say about the tongue too. You might want to study James later to see what the New Testament says about this subject.

DAY THREE

List what you learned from marking references to the Lord. Note the repetition of *abomination,*[13] and mark each reference with a black rectangle. This is a good word to mark throughout your Bible so you see what God considers an abomination. God's character never changes, so an abomination to Him thousands of years ago is still an abomination to Him today.

Determine the theme of Proverbs 15 and record it on PROVERBS AT A GLANCE.

DAY FOUR

Read Proverbs 16 today, marking the key words on your bookmark.

Also mark *pride,* and look for the contrasting attitude and mark it in a different way. Add these to your bookmark.

DAY FIVE

As you did for Proverbs 15, list what you learned about the results of what you say.

List what you learn about pride. Then go back to Proverbs 15:25 and add to your list what you learn there. Oh, what an important subject pride is in the Bible! Proverbs is just one of the books that addresses this topic.

DAY SIX

Today, list what you learn about the Lord, His concerns, what He controls, and what He thinks about certain actions and thoughts. Knowing God, His heart, His thoughts, His ways, and His power should help us love and reverence Him more and more. His ways are just. He's unchanging in His love, His mercy, and His just judgment of wickedness.

Don't forget to determine a theme for Proverbs 16 and record it on PROVERBS AT A GLANCE.

DAY SEVEN

Store in your heart: Proverbs 15:1; 16:18
Read and discuss: Proverbs 15–16

QUESTIONS FOR DISCUSSION OR INDIVIDUAL STUDY

∾ Discuss the role of the mouth and the consequences of what you say.

∽ What does the Lord think about the various actions you observed?

∽ What is the connection between pride and reproof?

∽ What things are abominations to the Lord and why?

∽ How can a man preserve his life?

∽ Review what you've learned throughout Proverbs about the wise and the foolish.

THOUGHT FOR THE WEEK

What does pride do to a person? One proverb says it precedes personal destruction and stumbling (a fall). But Proverbs also says the Lord will tear down the *house* of the proud. About 140 years after Solomon's reign, Uzziah, the tenth king of Judah, did right in the sight of the Lord, seeking God in the days of Isaiah. The Word says as long as he sought God, he prospered. He was successful in war because God helped him. His fame spread far and wide. (You can read his story in 2 Chronicles 26.)

But he later became proud, rejecting the truth that his success was due to the Lord's favor and opting to believe it was his own doing. And he stumbled.

Uzziah went into the temple of Solomon and decided to offer incense before God. For this, God struck him with leprosy for the rest of his life. He could no longer enter the temple because of this uncleanness and had to live apart from other people for the rest of his life.

What a tragedy! Such success followed by such a fall! But this is what Solomon was warning his son about in these proverbs. If he, his son, his grandson, and so on down the line had read, understood, and obeyed these proverbs, Uzziah might have acted differently.

Or perhaps not. Pride is like that—it blinds us to truth. The Hebrew word translated *pride* in Proverbs 16:18 is sometimes translated *swelling* or *exaltation*. We can almost see the swelled head, thinking more of itself than it ought, exalting itself when it ought to exalt the Lord. Pride in this chapter is not relative to other men but to God.

Pride began with the devil. As you read Ezekiel 28:12-17, you see that pride caused the fall of the "anointed cherub who covers" in Eden. Instead of exalting God for creating his beauty, he was "lifted up because of [his] beauty" and "corrupted [his] wisdom by reason of [his] splendor."

Pride spread to man in Eden as the devil enticed him to doubt God's Word and God's love. Appealing to man's own desire, Satan convinced man he could be like God by eating the forbidden fruit.

And man fell.

There is a simple cure for pride: God humbles us. Every single proud person is headed for God's humiliation. Adam and Eve were humbled by nakedness, by expulsion from Eden, by pain in childbirth, by toil to reap crops from their land, and by death.

Even if we're not humbled harshly within our lifetimes, we're ultimately humbled by death. No man cheats this final blow. And after it comes judgment, another thing no man escapes. The proud who have never believed God's gospel will see their fall throughout eternity.

The boastful pride of life is from the world, not from the Father, John tells us. Both James and Peter tell us that God is opposed to the proud but gives grace to the humble. The proud follow Satan's old trick, the snare that brings them down and that brought man down from the beginning.

It's possibly Satan's number one deceit, "Look at what *you* accomplished!"

When we succumb to this thought, when we mistake our own achievements for the good favor of the Lord, we fall into the snare Satan set for us and head for a fall.

So we must remember the proverb, the example of King Uzziah, and the teaching of John, James, and Peter. Obey God's Word and avoid the inevitable stumbling, fall, and destruction that follow pride.

It's Not What You Say, but What You Don't Say

Many things we say get us into trouble. Proverbs has taught us a lot about this already. In a complementary way, it teaches us to consider the effects of our words, to respond slowly, and sometimes to choose to say nothing.

DAY ONE

Read Proverbs 17 today, marking the key words on your bookmark. Take your time; don't rush. Let the truths of this chapter sink in as you read and mark these words. Don't miss *evil*.[14]

As we have seen for many chapters, the wise and the foolish are central characters, so list what you learn from marking these key words.

DAY TWO

Back in chapter 10, we began looking at the effect of the mouth—what we say and how we say it. This theme continues in chapter 17, but a new aspect arises. Read through the chapter again and note how often it refers to not speaking. List what you learn about remaining silent.

Continuing our pattern, formulate a theme for Proverbs 17 and record it on PROVERBS AT A GLANCE.

DAY THREE

Read Proverbs 18 today, marking the key words on your bookmark. Add to your lists what you learn about the contrasts between wisdom[15] and foolishness, the wise and the fool.

DAY FOUR

Proverbs 18:10 is probably familiar, but doesn't it seem out of place among verses that discuss wisdom, foolishness, and the effects of words? Consider why it appears here. One observation principle we learned in earlier chapters is to look for parallels—verses that reinforce a theme by using equivalent or contrasting ideas. Look at verses 10-12 and note what you learn.

Another theme in this chapter is the contrast between wealth and poverty. Record what you learn about this topic in chapter 18.

Finally, determine a theme for Proverbs 18 and record it on PROVERBS AT A GLANCE.

DAY FIVE

Read Proverbs 19 today, marking the key words on your bookmark.

Looking at what you marked, what seems to be the dominant theme in this chapter? How many verses speak to this issue?

Make a list of all you learn about wealth and poverty and related topics like generosity, gifts, and luxury. Mark *wealth*[16] with a dollar sign (or the symbol for the currency of your country) and add it to your bookmark.

DAY SIX

Yesterday, you spent some time learning about poverty and wealth, and we asked how important this subject is in chapter 19. Now, how do these things relate to the fool?

Determine a theme for Proverbs 19 and record it on PROVERBS AT A GLANCE.

DAY SEVEN

 Store in your heart: Proverbs 18:10

Read and discuss: Proverbs 17:4-14,27-28; 18:6-8,13, 19,24; 19:1,4-17

QUESTIONS FOR DISCUSSION OR INDIVIDUAL STUDY

∾ Review what you learned in Proverbs so far about the words you say.

∾ Discuss what these verses say about speaking and not speaking.

∾ What do all the other things you've learned about your speech tell you about the one who "conceals a transgression"? Explain.

 ∾ How can a friend love at all times? How does this relate to a friend who sticks closer than a brother?

 ∾ How would you apply Proverbs 18:10 to the subjects in these chapters?

 ∾ What did you learn about working diligently?

 ∾ Summarize and discuss the main themes of these chapters.

THOUGHT FOR THE WEEK

American humorist, novelist, short story author, and wit Mark Twain once wrote, "It is better to keep your mouth closed and let people think you are a fool than to open it and remove all doubt." While humorous, this saying rings true. Common wisdom is often based on God's Word; most people just don't know the original source.

These chapters of Proverbs deal with the same idea— keeping your mouth shut. Proverbs 17:28 says, "Even a fool, when he keeps silent, is considered wise; when he closes his lips, he is considered prudent." Not saying foolish things makes you seem wise; opening your mouth and saying foolish things proves you're a fool. Not speaking at all takes away the risk of accidentally speaking foolishness. So overall, silence is for your own good.

Another good reason for not speaking is that it can promote the good of others. For example, "Better is a dry morsel and quietness with it than a house full of feasting with strife" (Proverbs 17:1). In other words, a feast is not worth living with strife; peace and quietness are more valuable, even if you don't get much to eat or even if the food stinks. So too is quiet when a man sins. Trumpeting failures doesn't undo the sin, nor does it build unity or friendship. It separates. And Ephesians urges us to maintain the unity of the Spirit.

Allowing a quarrel to escalate into strife is like poking a hole in a dike or dam—before long, greater disaster arises. Sometimes the best decision is to keep quiet, keep the peace, and prevent a bigger mess. This is hard to do sometimes. We get the urge to speak up, speak out, speak our mind, tell the world what they need to know. But do they really need to know?

And what about our motives? Do we speak to get even? Do we spout off things in order to heal or to hurt? Will our words help hearers grow closer to God, or will they drive wedges between them and God, them and us, them and others?

Jesus spoke about this principle when He discussed church discipline (Matthew 18:15-18):

> If your brother sins, go and show him his fault in private; if he listens to you, you have won your brother. But if he does not listen to you, take one or two more with you, so that by the mouth of two or three witnesses every fact may be confirmed. If he refuses to listen to them, tell it to the church; and if he refuses to listen even to the church, let him be to you as a Gentile and a tax collector. Truly I say to you, whatever you bind on earth shall have been bound in heaven; and whatever you loose on earth shall have been loosed in heaven.

See? If he listens, you have won your brother. No separation. Share information privately—no tattling or gossip. Include others only if your brother refuses to acknowledge truth in the face of witnesses to the truth, and even then, do it in an orderly, regulated dispersion—a slow fanning out.

This is the friend who loves at all times, the brother born for adversity. In tough times, a cool spirit and restrained words suppress strife and produce harmony—prudent ways to right wrongs and correct those who have strayed. This is the kind of rebuke people listen to.

Yes, this kind of restraint leaves burdens in our heart we can't share with others. But we *can* share them with the Lord. We don't carry the burdens alone, and we don't have to carry them at all if we surrender them to the Lord in prayer. We live by the wisdom of God when we hold our tongues for the sake of others according to these Proverbs.

Compare Paul's admonition to the Philippians:

> Do nothing from selfishness or empty conceit,
> but with humility of mind regard one another as
> more important than yourselves; do not merely
> look out for your own personal interests, but also
> for the interests of others (Philippians 2:3-4).

One way to live this out is to consider *what* you say, *when* you say it, *how* you say it, and *to whom* you say it. Proverbs gives us godly wisdom in all these areas.

RICH MAN, POOR MAN

Proverbs 22:2 teaches us that "the rich and the poor have a common bond, the LORD is the maker of them all." So, are wealthy people and poor people really any different? Does God love wealthy people more than He loves poor people? Does this perspective of the sovereignty of God over all people help us stop coveting and currying the favor of the rich as assets and despising and avoiding the poor as liabilities?

DAY ONE

Read Proverbs 20 and mark the key words on your bookmark. Although *poor* is used only once in this chapter, there are several references to commerce or making money. Don't miss them! God provides wisdom for every area of our lives.

DAY TWO

What did you learn about wealth and poverty? List the points.

What relationship exists between wealth, poverty, and honesty? What does the Lord think about these?

Record a theme for Proverbs 20 on PROVERBS AT A GLANCE.

DAY THREE

Read Proverbs 21, marking the key words on your bookmark. You'll see that the subject of commerce, making a living, and handling wealth continues in this chapter.

DAY FOUR

Continue listing what you learn about wealth. Also record what you learn about the wicked and about evil.

Record a theme for Proverbs 21 on PROVERBS AT A GLANCE.

DAY FIVE

Read Proverbs 22, marking the key words from your bookmark. Again, note what this chapter teaches about wealth and poverty.

DAY SIX

Review all you have recorded about wealth this week, and see if you can summarize it into a few basic principles.

Read Proverbs 22:17-21 again and note the personal address. Relate this to the early chapters of Proverbs. What's the connection?

Record your theme for Proverbs 22 on PROVERBS AT A GLANCE.

DAY SEVEN

Store in your heart: Proverbs 22:1

Read and discuss: Proverbs 20:10-14,21-23; 21:13-17; 22:1-9,16,22-23,26-27

QUESTIONS FOR DISCUSSION OR INDIVIDUAL STUDY

- ∾ Discuss the contrast between wealth and poverty.

- ∾ What are the relationships between the righteous, the wicked, and wealth?

- ∾ What is God's view of honesty? Cite some examples.

- ∾ Discuss speech and knowledge as they relate to the behavior of the rich and the poor.

THOUGHT FOR THE WEEK

"Rich man, poor man, beggar man, thief" is a line from a children's rhyme, but our responsibility toward wealth is not child's play. God is serious about how we live, work, acquire wealth, and treat the poor. In our study of Proverbs 17–22 over the last two weeks, we have seen many references to wealth, to poverty, and to the treatment of the poor. These things reflect our relationship to the Lord.

"He who mocks the poor taunts his Maker," Proverbs 17:5 says. See how this fits with Proverbs 22:2? God makes both rich and poor; both are His creatures, so mocking them is mocking God. *Being* poor is not a sin, but *mocking* poor people is.

More important to God than riches, though, is the heart. "Better is a poor man who walks in his integrity than he who is perverse in speech and is a fool" (Proverbs 19:1). Here is the real key to a right relationship with God: character. Wealth doesn't measure godliness; character, integrity, and speech do. "He who is gracious to a poor man lends to the LORD, and He will repay him for his good deed…What is desirable in a man is his kindness, and it is better to be a poor man than a liar" (Proverbs 19:17,22).

The quest for wealth drives men to all sorts of evil. Paul wrote Timothy, "Those who want to get rich fall into temptation and a snare and many foolish and harmful desires which plunge men into ruin and destruction. For the love of money is a root of all sorts of evil, and some by longing for it have wandered away from the faith and pierced themselves with many griefs" (1 Timothy 6:9-10). He tells Timothy to flee from these things. Why? Because character, integrity, and devotion to the Lord are more important! God makes both the rich and the poor. We should seek not the wealth of the world but the wealth of godliness.

Jesus taught this in His Sermon on the Mount: You can't serve God and money, so don't store up treasures on earth where moth and rust destroy and where thieves break in and steal. Rather, store up treasures in heaven. Where your treasure is, there your heart will be also.

God's Word never changes. Jesus taught God's Word about the rich and the poor; Paul also taught God's Word about the rich and the poor. Both taught the wisdom Solomon taught his son, God's Word on the rich and the poor.

Wealth on earth is not the goal of the wise but rather of the fool who sacrifices his imperishable relationship to God for something that perishes, something he can't take with him when he leaves this world.

God does teach us to be good stewards of what He gives us. Jesus taught parables about faithful servants. We are stewards of our time, talents, and spiritual gifts as well as material things, and God gives us what we have among all these assets. He makes the rich and the poor. We are simply stewards of what God gives us. Our greatest reward is to hear Him say, "Well done, good and faithful servant."

WHO HAS WOE?
WHO HAS SORROW?

Those who linger long over drink receive woe and sorrow, contentions, complaining, wounds without cause, and red eyes. Oh, don't get me wrong; others get these things—it's just that drunkenness brings them on faster. Proverbs teaches us one simple way to avoid them.

DAY ONE

Read Proverbs 23 today, marking the key words from your bookmark. Make sure to mark *wealth*.[17]

DAY TWO

Read Proverbs 23 again, marking *rejoice* with a pink cloud shaded pink and *woe* with a black cloud shaded brown. Add these to your bookmark. In verses 1-21, mark *do not* and list the things Solomon warns us not to do.

DAY THREE

Read verses 20-35 again and list all the truths about drinking wine. This is the first passage we have seen about drinking alcohol. This can be a controversial subject in the church, and people have strong opinions about it. See if you can discern the main point about drinking wine here. Is the main point abstention, or is it self-control?

Record a theme for Proverbs 23 on PROVERBS AT A GLANCE.

DAY FOUR

Read Proverbs 24 and mark the words on your bookmark. Mark *curse*[18] with an orange cloud shaded brown and add it to your bookmark.

DAY FIVE

Read chapter 24 again and list what you learn about the contrast between the wise and the evil (wicked).

What does the chapter teach about honesty and mercy? God is just and honest; the devil is the liar and full of deceit. God is merciful; the devil is a murderer. So when we see what God teaches about honesty and mercy, He's simply showing us how to live a life that reflects our Father's character.

DAY SIX

List what you learn about God from this chapter. Your life can reflect your Father's character only if you are getting to know Him more and more. Knowing God—not just knowing about Him—and knowing His ways are the keys to living life according to His desires for us.

Read verses 30-34 and list what you learn about laziness.

Record a theme for Proverbs 24 on PROVERBS AT A GLANCE.

DAY SEVEN

Store in your Heart: Proverbs 23:17

Read and discuss: Proverbs 23:20-35; 24:12,23-29

QUESTIONS FOR DISCUSSION OR INDIVIDUAL STUDY

- Discuss what Proverbs 23 says about associating with heavy drinkers of wine and lingering over wine.

- What do you learn about God in chapter 24? What is the Lord's reaction to people who don't show mercy?

- Discuss what you learned about honesty in Proverbs 24.

- What do these chapters teach you about what to speak? What different ways can you use words?

- How do people react to honesty and speaking honestly? Do you identify with what Proverbs teaches?

THOUGHT FOR THE WEEK

"The Bible doesn't say anything about drinking!" he bellowed—he with the bloated face, the rumpled shirt, the perspiration when it wasn't hot, and the defense when no one was accusing. "Yes, it does," I replied. "It says not to be drunk!"

Drinking is a hot topic in Christian circles. On one side are teetotalers, who never touch alcohol. On the other side are those who drink to varying degrees. "Liberty!" one side cries out. "Testimony!" the other preaches. Sometimes the discussion devolves into accusations of legalism and censure of those who decry drinking.

Two things are true: Of those who are drunkards, 100 percent drink. Of those who are non-drinkers, 0 percent are drunkards. Vacuous argument, you might say. But one guarantee against drunkenness is not drinking.

We saw two interesting Proverbs that discuss drinking last week: "Wine is a mocker, strong drink a brawler, and whoever is intoxicated by it is not wise" (Proverbs 20:1), and "He who loves wine and oil will not become rich" (Proverbs 21:17).

In this week's study, Proverbs 23 informs us about the consequences of one who lingers over strong drink: contentions, complaints, wounds without cause, red eyes, strange sightings, perverse words, and cravings for more drink in the morning.

Now, what does the rest of the Bible say about drinking? What stories and teachings give us principles to understand?

Genesis 9 continues Noah's story after the flood. One day he became very drunk and uncovered himself in his tent. One of his sons, Ham, saw his father naked and reported it to his brothers instead of covering him. For this he was cursed. This scenario might not have occurred if Noah had not been drunk.

Genesis 19 tells the story of Lot and his two daughters following the destruction of Sodom and Gomorrah. They made their father so drunk he did not know he was having sex with them. The children produced were Moab and Ammon, whose descendants have plagued Israel to this day.

In Leviticus 10, God tells Aaron and his sons not to approach the tent of meeting if they have had wine or strong drink in order to make a distinction between the holy and profane.

In Isaiah 5:8-13, people who seek wine for pleasure are examples of God's people who will go into exile for lack of knowledge.

God uses drunkenness and its consequences (nakedness and vomit) as metaphors of arrogance, pride, and judgment—Moab in Jeremiah 48:26, Babylon in Jeremiah 51:7,39,57, Edom in Lamentations 4:21, and Nineveh in Nahum 3:11 are examples.

The Bible never bans drinking, but drunkenness is frequently contrasted with godliness and God-honoring behavior. All the consequences of being drunk are negative.

In the New Testament, the classic verse is Ephesians 5:18: "And do not get drunk with wine, for that is dissipation, but be filled with the Spirit."

The Greek word translated "dissipation" *(asotia)* means a wasteful spending or diversion of effort. The word is used in only two other places, both with negative senses:

> If any man is above reproach, the husband of one wife, having children who believe, not accused of dissipation or rebellion (Titus 1:6).

> In all this, they are surprised that you do not run with them into the same excesses of dissipation, and they malign you (1 Peter 4:4).

Dissipation (wasting) is a consequence of drunkenness, and it's always a bad quality.

First Timothy contains leadership qualities for elders and deacons that include "not...addicted to much wine" (3:8).

On the other hand, drinking itself is not condemned in Scripture. Paul even told Timothy to take a little wine for the sake of his stomach: "No longer drink water exclusively, but use a little wine for the sake of your stomach and your frequent ailments" (1 Timothy 5:23).

Romans 14 makes clear that wine itself is not unclean or evil, and Scripture includes no prohibition against drinking. But drunkenness is clearly evil. Drunkenness is the problem, and we're told not to associate with any drunk "brothers":

> I wrote you not to associate with any so-called
> brother if he is an immoral person, or covetous,
> or an idolater, or a reviler, or a drunkard, or
> a swindler—not even to eat with such a one
> (1 Corinthians 5:11).

And we learn that drunkards are among "the unrighteous" who will not inherit the kingdom of God:

> Or do you not know that the unrighteous will
> not inherit the kingdom of God? Do not be
> deceived; neither fornicators, nor idolaters, nor
> adulterers, nor effeminate, nor homosexuals,
> nor thieves, nor the covetous, nor drunkards,
> nor revilers, nor swindlers, will inherit the
> kingdom of God (1 Corinthians 6:9-10).

Drink is not evil, but drunkenness is. If you choose to drink, don't become drunk.

ℐPPLES
OF 𝒢OLD

Words matter. They can be apples of gold in silver settings like fine gold earrings or other ornaments. They can make things better and have the power to produce life...but only if they're wise words.

DAY ONE

Read Proverbs 25 and mark the words on your bookmark. Also mark *king* and *glory* and add them to your bookmark. Think about the two kinds of glory—God's and your own—and which one you desire the most.

DAY TWO

Read verse 1 and make note of the start of a new segment. Whose proverbs are these? Who recorded them? Mark this on PROVERBS AT A GLANCE.

If you're not familiar with Hezekiah, king of Judah, read 2 Kings 18:1-8. If you are interested in the whole story and have the time, read 2 Kings 18–20 and 2 Chronicles 29–32.

The main point is that Hezekiah brought the kingdom of Judah back to the Lord in the face of Assyria's threat after Assyria took the northern kingdom (Israel) captive.

DAY THREE

List what you learn about *glory* in this chapter. Make sure you note whose glory is mentioned—God's, the king's, or yours. Think again about the question we considered in day one. Whose glory do you desire the most?

Also list what you learn about words.

Write your theme for Proverbs 25 on PROVERBS AT A GLANCE.

DAY FOUR

Read Proverbs 26 and mark the key words. Mark *hate (hatred)*[19] and add it to your bookmark. You could mark it with a black heart, or you could draw a red heart with a black slash through it.

List what you learn about hate. Hatred itself is not bad. God says in Malachi that He hates divorce. The important thing is hating the right things. Think of the relationship between love and hate. Is there a middle ground?

DAY FIVE

List what you learn about fools in Proverbs 26. Note the reference to a proverb in the mouth of a fool.

If you didn't notice the repetition of *wise in his own eyes*, mark it now and list what you learn.

DAY SIX

List what you learn about laziness from what is said about the sluggard. If you don't know what a sluggard is, the context should make it clear.

What do you learn about the whisperer? Of course, this passage is not talking about speaking in a whisper. It's referring to what the whisperer is trying to accomplish. What is the whisperer doing?

Record the theme of Proverbs 26 on PROVERBS AT A GLANCE.

DAY SEVEN

 Store in your heart: Proverbs 25:11
Read and discuss: Proverbs 25:11-15,23-25; 26:1-12

QUESTIONS FOR DISCUSSION OR INDIVIDUAL STUDY

- ∞ Discuss what you learned about the effect of words.

- ∞ How is *your* speech? What would you like to change?

- ∞ What do you learn about fools in Proverbs 26?

- ∞ How does this compare to what you learned earlier in Proverbs? What do you remember?

ი What does *wise in your own eyes* mean? Where is wisdom found according to Proverbs?

ი What can you apply to your lives from Proverbs 25–26?

THOUGHT FOR THE WEEK

Proverbs 16:24 says, "Pleasant words are a honeycomb, sweet to the soul and healing to the bones." In the past few weeks we have looked at the power of good and bad words and their effects on people. This week we looked at right words in right circumstances—*well-chosen* words.

Too often in life we find ourselves using words inadequately. We don't know what to say in some situations. We find ourselves incapable of verbally expressing how we think and feel. Just think about stressful situations you've experienced, such as serious illnesses and deaths of family members and close friends—perhaps even in prayer you couldn't find words deep enough to express what was in your heart.

Here is the beauty of knowing the Word of God. Although some would dismiss verses you quote as trite, remember, they are God's words to us. They are meant to comfort, to uplift, to bring us truth, healing, and hope. Knowing the wisdom of God and speaking it in the right place and time is never trite, never commonplace, never wrong. The key is the right word in the right place at the right time.

Such are the gold apples in silver settings. Well-chosen words from God's Word, God's wisdom, are like fine pieces of jewelry that make every situation better because they bring comfort, healing, and hope.

Even God's words of reproof in the right place at the right time are like fine jewelry. But how can this be? How can showing people they're wrong adorn or beautify like jewelry?

These words bring wanderers back from destruction, from judgment, from receiving wrath for wrong thoughts, words, and deeds.

Criticism can beautify? Think about it. When your children do something dangerous, you don't hesitate to tell them to stop, snatch them away from the danger, and then explain to them how their actions could have been harmful. God does the same for His children. He summed up His guides to life and cautions of dangers in a book for us to learn from and use. If we realize His wisdom is superior to ours and we know His words are designed to help and never hurt us, why wouldn't we share them even if they sound critical to some people?

Proverbs 25:13 likens the faithfully delivered message to refreshment for the soul. We'll see this theme repeated in Proverbs 27, so look for it there too. Here are two principles to watch for: Open criticism is better than concealed love, and the critique of a friend is faithful.

Words spoken rightly are beneficial, not harmful. Even if your immediate reaction is to feel hurt, if they are right words according to God's Word and delivered in the right way at the right time, they won't be harmful. In time, you'll recognize them as for your own good.

But how do we know how, when, and what to say? Know God's wisdom first. Pray that God brings healing words to your mind and opportunities to deliver them at right times in the right way.

I've had a few cases of people saying they were "speaking the truth in love"—and perhaps they were—but I can guarantee they weren't at the right time. In the midst of a situation not going as smoothly as planned, telling someone, "You should have done this or that" probably won't help. After things have calmed down and people are thinking through the situation dispassionately, they can receive helpful correction without irritation. I'm sure I've done the same thing, and I'll bet you have too. What we failed to do was hit the timing right. We leaped into the situation without God's timing; the circumstances were wrong for the delivery of the right message. That's where prayer plays a key role.

So pray. Ask God to show you what to say and when to say it—how to deliver gold apples in silver settings.

WISE IN HIS OWN EYES

The rich man is wise in his own eyes, but the poor man with understanding sees right through him. This isn't a statement about rich or poor people, but about wisdom and understanding. God's wisdom is different from our own. The one who has God's wisdom can see right through the one who is wise in his own eyes.

DAY ONE

Read Proverbs 27 today, marking the key words on your bookmark. Mark *wrath*[20] with an orange *W* and add it to your bookmark.

List what you learn about riches from verses 23-27.

DAY TWO

As in previous chapters, make a list of what you learned about *what* to say, *who* to say it to, *when* to say it, and *how* to say it.

What makes a heart glad?

Record a theme for Proverbs 27 on PROVERBS AT A GLANCE.

DAY THREE

Read Proverbs 28, marking the words on your bookmark. *Prayer* and *compassion*[21] are worth marking and noting though they each appear only once. Mark *prayer* with a purple bowl shaded pink. The prayers of the saints are like incense before God (Revelation 8:3-4). Shade *compassion* green. You don't need to add these to your bookmark.

DAY FOUR

List what you learn about the poor and the rich, noting especially the contrasts.

Also note contrasts between the righteous and wicked. (You may want to make a two-column list to make this contrast clear.)

Decide a theme for Proverbs 28 and record it on PROVERBS AT A GLANCE.

DAY FIVE

Read Proverbs 29 and mark the key words on your bookmark. We're nearly at the end of Proverbs! Keep up the good work. Don't give up—the goal is close!

DAY SIX

Again, the contrasts between the wicked and righteous[22] are key in this chapter. You may want to add what you learn in this chapter to the list you made from Proverbs 28.

Also list what you learn about the wise and wisdom.

Record a theme for Proverbs 29 on PROVERBS AT A GLANCE.

DAY SEVEN

 Store in your heart: Proverbs 27:6

Read and discuss: Proverbs 27:1-9; 28:3-16,23; 29:1-13,16

QUESTIONS FOR DISCUSSION OR INDIVIDUAL STUDY

- Discuss the contrasts between the wicked and the righteous.

- What are the consequences of wicked behavior?

- What kinds of behavior bring about blessing and rejoicing?

- Relate experiences you have had that confirm these truths.

- How does confessing and forsaking transgressions bring about compassion? How does concealing them work against compassion?

- How does understanding enable you to see through those who are wise in their own eyes?

THOUGHT FOR THE WEEK

Seeking the Lord brings understanding, and understanding helps us see through those who are wise in their own eyes. Those without understanding just don't get it! They think no one will see their transgressions. They think they'll get away with their behavior.

Proverbs says this won't happen. Oppressors will oppress, but they won't prosper. Oh, they may prosper financially for a time, accumulating riches of this world that moths eat and rust destroys. But they won't take those riches with them.

In the Sermon on the Mount, Jesus teaches His disciples to store up treasures in heaven. He tells them that wherever their treasure is, their hearts will be too. We can't take material wealth with us, so spiritual things like integrity, honesty, mercy, and justice matter more. These things reflect God's character. Proverbs 28:6 says being poor and walking in integrity is better than being rich and crooked. Proverbs 27:19 summarizes that our hearts reflect what we are just as water reflects a face. Our manner of living, ruling, gaining wealth...all these reflect our hearts.

Why is integrity better than crookedness? Because God judges our deeds, not our possessions. First Corinthians 3:8-15 links our rewards in heaven to our deeds (not how much we owned) on earth. In his letter to Titus, Paul cautions us to do good deeds out of duty (2:7,14; 3:8,14). But in 1 Corinthians, Paul adds the idea of heavenly rewards. First Corinthians 4:2-5 adds that God counts and judges the motives attached to our deeds as well. We can do the same deed for God's glory or for our own—big difference!

In fact, 1 Corinthians 3:15 says we can suffer loss because of the very quality (not quantity) of our work. Quality includes motives—the reasons *why* we do things, which reside in our hearts and reflect what we are.

Paul expanded this idea for the Corinthians when he gave them details about the judgment seat of Christ:

> For we must all appear before the judgment seat of Christ, so that each one may be recompensed for his deeds in the body, according to what he has done, whether good or bad (2 Corinthians 5:10).

None of this New Testament teaching is new. Solomon's wisdom in Proverbs taught exactly these things nearly a thousand years before Jesus preached and Paul wrote.

Proverbs 25:21-22 says the Lord will reward us for feeding our enemies and giving them something to drink when they're hungry and thirsty.

Proverbs 24:12 tells us the Lord weighs hearts and renders to man according to his work.

So what shall we do with Proverbs? Acknowledge it as God's Word and live by it, or treat it like Benjamin Franklin's *Poor Richard's Almanac*? Does it sum up man's temporal experiences or God's eternal wisdom? The Bible claims that true wisdom is from God. Proverbs is God's wisdom to and for us.

Do we trust God? Do we believe God's Word? Shall we live by it? What did Jesus do?

*A*N *E*XCELLENT *W*IFE

Thank God, the search for the perfect mate today is now computerized—efficient and perfect! In addition to computer profiling, people make use of personal dating services, matchmaking, and speed dating. Years ago marriages were arranged (they still are in some parts of the world). What are people looking for?

If you want to know God's idea for the "power woman" (Hebrew, *isheh hayil*—Proverbs 31:10), read Proverbs 31.

DAY ONE

Read Proverbs 30:1 and note whose proverbs these are. You might want to mark this in some special way on PROVERBS AT A GLANCE.

Then read Proverbs 30, marking the key words on your bookmark.

DAY TWO

List what you learned from marking references to God. How do these truths relate to the author of this chapter?

Read Proverbs 30:10-14 again and underline the phrase *there is a kind*.[23] What are the four kinds of man?

DAY THREE

Read Proverbs 30:15-33 again and underline *three things* and *four*. Number each of the four things in the text. This expression, "three things and four," also occurs in the minor prophet Amos. The Old Testament uses a number and then the next higher number as a literary device. The higher number—in this case, four—is enumerated in detail with emphasis on the last item.

List the topics mentioned in each of these passages: verses 15-17, verses 18-20, verses 21-23, and verses 24-28.

How do these relate to what the author says about God in the first nine verses?

Finally, record a theme for Proverbs 30 on PROVERBS AT A GLANCE.

DAY FOUR

According to Proverbs 31:1, who's the author of this final chapter? Record this on PROVERBS AT A GLANCE.

Read Proverbs 31:1-9, marking the key words on your bookmark. Also mark references to *strong drink*[24] and *wine*. How do these proverbs relate to verse 1?

DAY FIVE

Now read Proverbs 31:10-31, marking the key words from your bookmark.

What's the main subject? This is probably one of the best-known passages in Proverbs and describes the excellent wife. This is a very appropriate way to end a book about life...about parents passing along to their children wisdom for living. What better thing to teach a son than how to choose his partner for life? And of course, this chapter teaches every woman how to be an excellent wife.

List the wife's characteristics. If you discern a common quality, note it.

DAY SIX

Review Proverbs 31:10-31, this time looking for how the excellent wife's virtues impact her husband and children.

How does verse 30 relate to what we've learned about wisdom throughout Proverbs? How is this a fitting end to the book?

Finally, record a theme for Proverbs 31 on PROVERBS AT A GLANCE.

DAY SEVEN

Store in your heart: Proverbs 31:30
Read and discuss: Proverbs 30:1-10; 31:10-31

QUESTIONS FOR DISCUSSION OR INDIVIDUAL STUDY

- ∞ Discuss Agur's words in Proverbs 30:1-10 in light of all you learned about wisdom from Proverbs.

- ∞ Discuss relationships between understanding, knowledge, and wisdom.

- ∞ How do you identify with Agur, and how do you differ?

- ∞ Discuss God's instructions about an excellent wife.

- ∞ If you're a woman, what applications can you make? What are some of your significant responsibilities?

- ∞ If you're a man, what applications can you make? And if you're married, how will these applications affect your relationship with your wife?

- ∞ What have you learned from this study of Proverbs that will impact your life? How will it affect your relationship with Almighty God?

- ∞ How will you acquire wisdom, understanding, and knowledge?

THOUGHT FOR THE WEEK

Charm is deceitful and beauty is vain, *but* a woman who fears the LORD, she shall be praised (Proverbs 31:30).

Does this one verse sum up what you learned in the past 13 weeks from Proverbs? If so, how? What if we add this verse:

Behold, for thus shall the man be blessed
Who fears the LORD (Psalm 128:4).

Do you see the principle? Whether you're a man or you're a woman, fear of the Lord brings praise and blessing. Out of the 25 verses the phrase "the fear of the Lord" appears in, 14 are in Proverbs. Why? Because the fear of the Lord is the beginning of wisdom.

If you make a list of all you learned about the fear of the Lord in Proverbs, you will be amazed. Fear of the Lord is the beginning of knowledge, the beginning of wisdom, the prolonger of life, the hatred of evil, the fountain of life, the confidence in life. It's rewards are riches, honor, and life.

Small wonder Proverbs gives us God's answers for today's problems. Most of all, we need knowledge and right application—wisdom. Just fearing the Lord is the beginning of these two things. But when we study God's Word, we gain *more* knowledge and wisdom. We gain confidence in knowing God through His Word to us. We gain the kinds of riches, honor, and life only God can give.

The world touts its own wisdom as the answer to life's problems. But the world's answers don't lead to eternal life; they don't lead to the honor God gives. They don't direct us toward the riches of grace poured out on us in Christ Jesus, the riches of the glory of His inheritance in the saints (Ephesians 1:18).

The world searches for happiness, but it can only find what's transient and fleeting. The answers to today's problems extend beyond this world and into the next; the world's answers are for this world only. If you prefer "Well done, good and faithful servant!" to "Depart from me, I never knew you!" when you stand before the Lord who made you, you're going to have to go beyond the world by observing, interpreting, and applying *God's* answers to today's problems. You need to know them, carry them about in your heart, apply them to your life, and live them out…starting now if you haven't already begun.

Before the children of Israel entered the promised land 3400 years ago, Moses summed up God's Law with this counsel on the plains of Moab:

> Now, Israel, what does the LORD your God require from you, but to fear the LORD your God, to walk in all His ways and love Him, and to serve the LORD your God with all your heart and with all your soul (Deuteronomy 10:12).

Proverbs gives us hundreds of practical applications of these three summary requirements from Deuteronomy. Jesus quoted from Proverbs over and over to show us that God's truth is timeless and His proverbs valid for today.

Make the proverbs your friends and constant companions. Read them over and over. Some people read a chapter a day from Proverbs, year after year. Memorize them. Live by them. Make God's answers for today's problems your answers.

Theme of Proverbs:

SEGMENT DIVISIONS

	MAIN DIVISIONS		CHAPTER THEMES
	THE CRY OF WISDOM, KNOWLEDGE, AND UNDERSTANDING	1	
		2	
		3	
		4	
		5	
		6	
		7	
		8	
		9	
	THE PROVERBS OF SOLOMON AND WISDOM OF WISE MEN	10	
		11	
		12	
		13	
		14	
		15	
		16	
		17	
		18	
		19	
		20	
		21	
		22	
		23	
		24	
	SOLOMON'S PROVERBS TRANSCRIBED	25	
		26	
		27	
		28	
		29	
	WORDS & COUNSEL OF OTHERS	30	
		31	

Author:

Date:

Purpose:

Key Words:

my son

wisdom (wise)

knowledge

understanding

fear

commandment(s)

instruction

tongue

fool (folly)

righteous

evil

wicked

NOTES

1. KJV: discerning
2. ESV: insight
3. KJV: strange woman; NKJV: immoral woman; ESV: forbidden woman
4. KJV: strange woman; NIV: wayward wife; NKJV: seductress; ESV: married woman
5. KJV: strange woman; NIV: wayward wife; NKJV: seductress
6. NIV: prostitute; ESV: prostitute
7. ESV: sense
8. NIV: judgment; ESV: insight
9. KJV, NKJV: foolish woman
10. KJV: just
11. NIV: evil conduct; NKJV: evil; ESV: wrong
12. NIV: correction; NKJV: correction, rebuke
13. NIV: detests
14. KJV: mischief; NIV: trouble; ESV: calamity
15. NIV, NKJV, ESV: judgment
16. KJV, NKJV: riches
17. KJV, NKJV, NIV: rich(es)
18. NIV: denounce
19. NIV: malice
20. NIV: anger
21. KJV, NIV, NKJV, ESV: mercy
22. KJV: just
23. KJV: there is a generation; NIV: those whose; NKJV: there is a generation; ESV: there are those
24. NIV: beer; NKJV: intoxicating drink

BOOKS IN THE
NEW INDUCTIVE STUDY SERIES

∾∾∾∾

Teach Me Your Ways
GENESIS, EXODUS,
LEVITICUS, NUMBERS, DEUTERONOMY

*Choosing Victory,
Overcoming Defeat*
JOSHUA, JUDGES, RUTH

Desiring God's Own Heart
1 & 2 SAMUEL, 1 CHRONICLES

Walking Faithfully with God
1 & 2 KINGS, 2 CHRONICLES

*Overcoming Fear
and Discouragement*
EZRA, NEHEMIAH, ESTHER

*Trusting God
in Times of Adversity*
JOB

*Praising God Through
Prayer and Worship*
PSALMS

*God's Answers for
Today's Problems*
PROVERBS

*Walking with God
in Every Season*
ECCLESIASTES, SONG OF SOLOMON,
LAMENTATIONS

Face-to-Face with a Holy God
ISAIAH

*God's Blueprint
for Bible Prophecy*
DANIEL

*Discovering the God
of Second Chances*
JONAH, JOEL, AMOS, OBADIAH

*Finding Hope
When Life Seems Dark*
HOSEA, MICAH, NAHUM,
HABAKKUK, ZEPHANIAH

*Opening the Windows
of Blessing*
HAGGAI, ZECHARIAH, MALACHI

The Coming of God's Kingdom
MATTHEW

Experiencing the Miracles of Jesus
MARK

The Call to Follow Jesus
LUKE

*The God Who Cares
and Knows You*
JOHN

*The Holy Spirit
Unleashed in You*
ACTS

*God's Answers for
Relationships and Passions*
1 & 2 CORINTHIANS

*Free from Bondage
God's Way*
GALATIANS, EPHESIANS

That I May Know Him
PHILIPPIANS, COLOSSIANS

*Standing Firm in
These Last Days*
1 & 2 THESSALONIANS

*Walking in Power,
Love, and Discipline*
1 & 2 TIMOTHY, TITUS

The Key to Living by Faith
HEBREWS

*Living with Discernment
in the End Times*
1 & 2 PETER, JUDE

God's Love Alive in You
1, 2, & 3 JOHN,
PHILEMON, JAMES

Behold, Jesus Is Coming!
REVELATION

NEW AMERICAN STANDARD BIBLE
UPDATED EDITION

THE *New* INDUCTIVE STUDY BIBLE

DISCOVERING THE TRUTH FOR YOURSELF

CHANGING THE WAY PEOPLE STUDY GOD'S WORD

"Inductive study of the Bible is the best way to discover scriptural truth...There is no jewel more precious than that which you have mined yourself."

—HOWARD HENDRICKS

Every feature is designed to help you gain a more intimate understanding of God and His Word. This study Bible, the only one based entirely on the inductive study approach, provides you with the tools for observing what the text says, interpreting what it means, and applying it to your life.